America's Leaders

The
SURGEON GENERAL

by Howard Gutner

BLACKBIRCH®
PRESS

THOMSON

GALE

San Diego • Detroit • New York • San Francisco • Cleveland • New Haven, Conn. • Waterville, Maine • London • Munich

Photo credits: Cover, back cover © Creatas; Alexander Hammond and Richard Carmona cover insets, pages 14, 19, 20, 24, 25, 29 © CORBIS; Everett Koop and Parklawn Building cover insets, pages 9, 10,11, 15, 17, 18, 21, 23, 28 © Department of Health and Human Services; page 7 © Réunion des Musées Nationaux / Art Resource, NY; pages 27, 31 © AP / Wide World Photos; pages 4, 5 © Blackbirch Press Archives; pages 6, 12 © Library of Congress; pages 8, 22 © Northwind Picture Archives; pages 13, 16 © PhotoDisc

LIBRARY OF CONGRESS CATALOGING-IN-PUBLICATION DATA

Gutner, Howard.
  The Surgeon General / by Howard Gutner.
    v. cm. — (America's leaders)
Includes bibliographical references and index.
Contents: Creation of the Marine Hospital Service — A growing responsibility — Responsibilities of the Surgeon General — Who works with the Surgeon General? — Where does the Surgeon General work? — Who can become Surgeon General? — A time of crisis — Another time of crisis — The Surgeon General's day.
  ISBN 1-56711-296-X (hbk. : alk. paper)
  1. United States. Public Health Service. Office of the Surgeon General—Juvenile literature. [1. United States. Public Health Service. Office of the Surgeon General.] I. Title. II. America's leaders series.

RA11.B19G88 2003
362.1'0973—dc21
                                                                    2002155066

Table of Contents

Creation of the Marine Hospital Service

More than 200 hundred years ago, a group of men wrote a document, the U.S. Constitution, which established the American government. The authors of the Constitution divided the government into three separate branches: the legislative branch, the judicial branch, and the executive branch. Under the Constitution, the leader of the executive branch was the president.

The Constitution gave the president the power to enforce existing laws. Only the legislative branch of the government, however, which includes the Senate and

The U.S. Constitution was drafted in 1789. It granted the federal government the ability to make new laws and offices to serve the citizens of the United States.

In 1798, President John Adams signed into law a bill that established the Marine Hospital Service. The service provided health care for sailors in the U.S. Navy.

the House of Representatives, can make new laws. Ideas for these laws come from many sources. Some come from the president or members of the legislative branch. Other ideas come from groups or even ordinary citizens.

If a senator is interested in an idea or a cause, it may become a bill. The bill then goes to the Senate for a vote. For the bill to become a law, it must be approved by both the Senate and the House of Representatives. It must also be signed by the president.

This marine hospital was built in San Francisco as part of the Marine Hospital Service Act. San Francisco and other port cities needed such hospitals because of their heavy U.S. Navy traffic.

In 1798, President John Adams signed into law a bill that grew out of concern for sailors in the U.S. Navy. Because sailors came from all over the country, and could get sick anywhere, their health care had become a challenge for the United States. If a sailor's ship docked in a city that he had never visited before, he might have trouble finding a good doctor. The bill Adams signed set up the Marine Hospital Service (MHS). After the law was passed, a number of marine hospitals were built, mainly in port cities, to care for sailors who were sick or injured.

When Adams was president, there were three departments in the executive branch to help him. These were the departments of state, treasury, and war. The leader of each department was called a secretary. Together, the secretaries formed a group known as the cabinet.

The Marine Hospital Service was made part of the Treasury Department. To raise money to pay doctors and build hospitals, American sailors were taxed 20 cents a month. The money was taken from ship captains by tax collectors in U.S. ports.

As this 19th-century painting shows, American harbors were busy places. Every sailor going ashore in U.S. ports paid a tax that supported the Marine Hospital Service.

A Growing Responsibility

In the early 1800s, contagious diseases often swept through the nation. Smallpox, yellow fever, and cholera killed many people, and spread panic and fear. Congress passed laws to try to stop the spread of these diseases. These new laws caused the purpose of the Marine Hospital Service to change. It still provided health care

This drawing depicts a yellow fever epidemic in the 1800s. Congress tried to halt the spread of disease by ordering doctors from marine hospitals to inspect all passengers on incoming ships.

to sailors, but now it also tried to stop the spread of disease throughout the country.

Doctors who worked for the Marine Hospital Service began to inspect ships as they came to the United States. They checked to make sure sailors were healthy before they were allowed back into the country.

The doctors also looked to see if there were animals, such as rats, that might carry disease onboard the

In 1871, President Ulysses S. Grant appointed John Maynard Woodworth (pictured) the first supervising surgeon of the Marine Hospital Service. The position was later renamed the surgeon general.

ships. Some doctors studied how epidemics started and spread from town to town.

In 1870, the Marine Hospital Service was reorganized by President Ulysses S. Grant. The job of supervising surgeon was created to run the service. Grant made John Maynard Woodworth, an army surgeon who had studied in Europe, the first supervising surgeon in 1871.

This 1905 photo shows doctors of the Commissioned Corps of the Marine Hospital Service. Like members of the military, the doctors wore uniforms and were sent around the country where needed.

Once he started his new job, Woodworth made some changes. He wanted to run the Marine Hospital Service in the same way the army and navy were run. He made the doctors who worked for the service wear uniforms. He also put together a group of doctors who would travel to marine hospitals across the country in an emergency. On January 4, 1889, Congress recognized Woodworth's new group and named it the Commissioned Corps. At first, the corps was made up of doctors alone. Over the years, however, the corps grew larger. It included dentists, nurses, and other health workers.

Many of these workers were needed as the duties of the Marine Hospital Service expanded again at the end of the 19th-century. In 1891, it became the federal government's job to admit immigrants to the country. The Marine Hospital Service got a new task: to do a medical check of immigrants at entry points such as Ellis Island in New York. Because of its new functions, the Marine Hospital Service was renamed the Public Health Service (PHS) in 1912. That same year, President William Howard Taft gave the supervising surgeon the title of surgeon general and put him in charge of the new Public Health Service.

In 1891, Marine Hospital Service members were called upon to inspect the health of newly arrived immigrants. Because of this new role, the service was renamed the Public Health Service in 1912.

The hospital on Ellis Island in New York Harbor was built in 1902. The Commissioned Corps doctors checked over the thousands of immigrants who arrived there daily.

The Public Health Service continued to grow throughout the 20th-century. In 1979, the PHS became part of the new and much larger Department of Health and Human Services. Today, the PHS is made up of the surgeon general and the Commissioned Corps, the Centers for Disease Control and Prevention, the Food and Drug Administration, and other agencies that work to keep Americans healthy.

Responsibilities of the Surgeon General

Since 1871, the surgeon general of the United States has been the nation's leading spokesperson on matters of public health. One of the duties of the surgeon general is to protect and advance the health of all U.S. citizens. To do this, he or she holds conferences and workshops to teach the public about health issues, such as smoking or the prevention of heart disease.

The Commissioned Corps works with the surgeon general to find health hazards in the environment and help fix them. It also makes sure that drugs and medical devices are safe and food is wholesome. It checks that cosmetics are harmless and electronic products do not expose people to dangerous radiation. In addition, it gives medical aid after disasters such as hurricanes or floods.

> **USA Fact**
> The budget for the Commissioned Corps is more than $600 million a year.

The Commissioned Corps works with the surgeon general to make sure prescription drugs are safe for use.

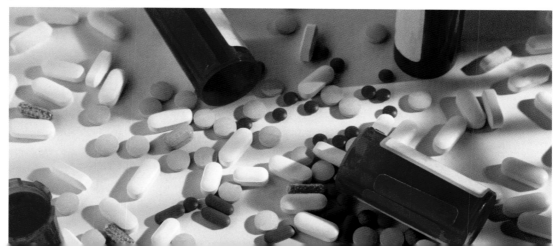

The surgeon general works with nations that have few doctors. Surgeon General David Satcher (rear, center) visited Africa in 2000 to consult on the AIDS crisis there.

The Commissioned Corps was set up to provide the American people with doctors and other health workers. As head of the Commissioned Corps, the surgeon general must provide health care to Native Americans, Native Alaskans, and other people who live in places that have few doctors. One other important part of the surgeon general's job is to work with other nations to solve global health problems.

Who Works with the Surgeon General?

The 6,000 officers of the Commissioned Corps all work in 1 of 11 types of jobs. Some work as dentists, pharmacists, dietitians, or physicians. Others are engineers, scientists, or environmental health professionals. The corps also has therapists, health service professionals, veterinarians, and nurses.

Each of these jobs or fields has a chief officer who is also a captain in the armed forces. Just as the president needs advisers to help run the executive branch, the surgeon general needs advisers in the Commissioned Corps.

Uniformed members of the Public Health Service's Commissioned Corps aided police and firefighters at the site of the New York World Trade Center after it was destroyed by terrorists in September 2001.

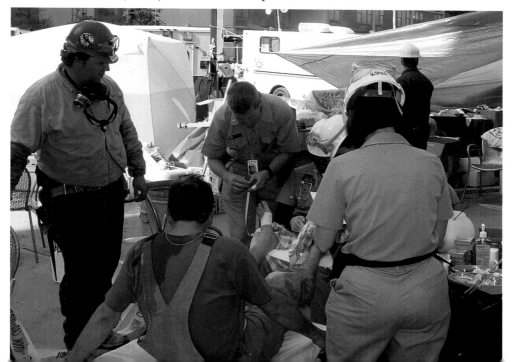

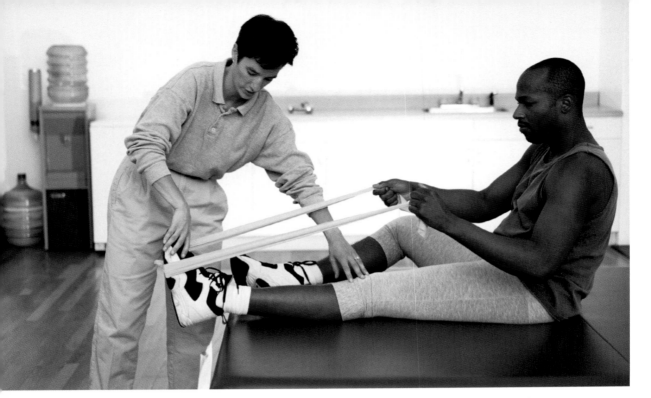

Physical therapy programs are among the many services offered by the Commissioned Corps.

All the chief officers report directly to the surgeon general. The chief dental officer, for example, oversees all dental programs for the PHS. These programs are put together for people who live in places that have few dentists. The chief therapist officer directs all speech and physical therapy programs for people who might otherwise not be able to afford them.

The surgeon general must get approval from the assistant secretary for health for any programs the Commissioned Corps wants to start.

Where Does the Surgeon General Work?

The office of the surgeon general, along with most other offices of the PHS, is located in the 18-story Parklawn Building in Rockville, Maryland. Rockville is a suburb of Washington, D.C. The Parklawn Building is part of a large complex of buildings that hold some offices of the Department of Health and Human Services. The Parklawn Building's three wings house 6,000 employees. They work in areas such as food and drugs, health education and services, and mental health.

The Parklawn Building in Rockville, Maryland, houses the offices of the surgeon general and the Public Health Service.

The Hubert H. Humphrey Building

As an officer in the Department of Health and Human Services, the surgeon general meets often with the assistant secretary for health. The headquarters of the U.S. Department of Health and Human Services is located in the Hubert H. Humphrey Building, at the foot of Capitol Hill in Washington, D.C

The Hubert H. Humphrey Building in Washington, D.C., houses the headquarters of the U.S. Department of Health and Human Services, which supervises the surgeon general's office.

Like every surgeon general, C. Everett Koop (pictured) made speeches and gave presentations to local communities about public health issues.

Outside of Washington

The surgeon general often travels to cities across the United States to make speeches and give presentations on public health issues. He or she may also meet with medical officials from other countries to discuss health concerns that affect the United States and the rest of the world.

Who Can Become Surgeon General?

The surgeon general is appointed by the president for a four-year term of office. The Senate must approve the person who is chosen by the president. The surgeon general reports to the assistant secretary for health. The assistant secretary is the main adviser to the secretary of the Department of Health and Human Services. Sixteen men and women have served as surgeon general.

To become surgeon general of the United States, a person must have a degree from a recognized medical school and at least one year of medical training at a hospital in the United States. A candidate for surgeon general must also have a license to practice medicine in at least 1 of the 50 states.

Surgeon General Leonard Scheele (left) led a discussion on polio prevention with Dr. Jonas Salk (right), the developer of polio vaccine, in 1955. All surgeon generals are appointed by the president and confirmed by the Senate.

A Time of Crisis

In the early years of the 20th century, Surgeon General Walter Wyman found himself in the middle of a crisis that involved bubonic plague in the city of San Francisco. Bubonic plague is spread by fleas that have bitten a rodent that carries the disease. It gets its name from lymph nodes in the neck and groin that swell when people get bubonic plague. These swollen nodes are known are buboes. People with plague also suffer from high fever, headache, and chills. A century ago, more than half of all people who came down with bubonic plague died. Today, it can be treated easily with antibiotics.

Walter Wyman

In the summer of 1899, a ship from Hong Kong arrived in San Francisco. Two people onboard had plague. Because of this, the ship was quarantined at San Francisco. When the boat was searched, 11 stowaways were found. The next day, 2 of them were missing. Their bodies were later found in San Francisco Bay.

An epidemic of bubonic plague hit San Francisco's Chinatown (pictured) in 1900. The surgeon general and the Commissioned Corps were able to stop the epidemic from spreading elsewhere.

When a doctor checked the bodies, he found signs of bubonic plague. Nine months later, in the spring of 1900, an epidemic of plague hit San Francisco.

At that time, Joseph Kinyoun was a Commissioned Corps doctor stationed in San Francisco. In April 1900, he was asked to look at the body of a worker who had died in the city's Chinatown section. Kinyoun soon realized that the man had died of bubonic plague.

Many local officials and business leaders, as well as people who lived in Chinatown, grew concerned.

They were afraid that news of the plague would harm their lives and businesses. They refused to believe that the worker had died of plague. They also refused to be quarantined.

Later that year, Wyman took action. He forced the governor of California not to let people from the state travel unless they had health certificates. The governor, however, convinced President William McKinley to lift the travel ban late in 1901.

By 1903, the situation in San Francisco had grown very serious. Many people were getting sick with the plague. Wyman called an emergency meeting in Washington, D.C. He said that all traffic between California and the rest of the country should be stopped unless the Commissioned Corps was allowed to get rid of the plague.

Rupert Blue

Faced with the threat of a national boycott, San Francisco officials finally agreed to help Wyman. A successful fight to stop the plague was led by Rupert Blue, who later went on to serve as surgeon general.

Another Time of Crisis

For years, many scientists and doctors knew that smoking might be bad for a person's health. It was not until the 1950s, however, that evidence was published in Great Britain that linked cigarette smoking to lung cancer and other diseases.

U.S. surgeon general Luther Terry (center) headed a government committee on smoking and human health. The committee reported in 1964 that smoking caused many diseases.

After Congress passed a law in 1965, all cigarette packages had to carry a warning from the surgeon general like these seen in this photo.

Soon after the report came out, Surgeon General Luther Terry formed a committee to write a similar report for the United States. Released on January 11, 1964, this report linked lung cancer and bronchitis to cigarette smoking. It also said that evidence showed smoking caused other problems, such as emphysema and heart disease.

Luther Terry's report made many tobacco companies angry. They feared they would lose money if a large number of people quit smoking. Many companies tried to find proof that smoking was not connected to disease. Despite their efforts, in 1965, Congress passed a law that required the surgeon general's warnings about smoking to be printed on all cigarette packs sold in America.

The Surgeon General's Day

As the person who must protect the health of all U.S. citizens, the surgeon general has a busy schedule, filled with meetings and public appearances. Here is what a day might be like for the surgeon general:

6:00 AM	Wake, shower, watch television news
6:30 AM	Eat breakfast
7:00 AM	At work in the Parklawn Building; meet with assistant surgeon general to preview the events for the day
8:00 AM	Meeting with the 11 chief officers who oversee the Commissioned Corps
10:00 AM	Work on report about the dangers of being overweight, with diet and exercise recommendations
12:00 PM	Interview with the host of a national radio talk show
1:00 PM	Working lunch with assistant secretary for health in the Hubert H. Humphrey Building to discuss the budget for the Commissioned Corps
2:30 PM	Appearance at a local high school to speak on the dangers of secondhand smoke

4:00 PM	Back at the surgeon general's office in the Parklawn Building; meet with a group of doctors from South Africa about the fight against AIDS in Africa
5:30 PM	Review report from the chief officer of environmental health
6:30 PM	Return home; eat dinner and watch evening news
7:30 PM	Handle pressing paperwork
8:30 PM	Phone call from assistant secretary of health and human services; discuss upcoming press conference on the surgeon general's report on diet, exercise, and the dangers of being overweight
9:30 PM	Phone call to the chief dietitian officer to ask for a report to be delivered in the morning
10:30 PM	Bed

The surgeon general has to keep informed about many different types of health hazards. Pictured are Surgeon General Richard Carmona (right) and Arizona governor Jane Hull (left) at a bioterrorism conference in 2002.

Fascinating Facts

Luther Terry

Luther Terry served as surgeon general from 1961 to 1965. After he left the post, he worked with groups such as the American Cancer Society. Terry helped stop television and radio advertisements for cigarettes. He also worked hard to make smoking in office buildings against the law.

John Maynard Woodworth, the first surgeon general, served from 1871 to 1879. When the Civil War began, he joined the Union army under General William Sherman. Woodworth was in charge of the ambulance train during Sherman's march through Georgia. He brought the sick and wounded to Savannah without the loss of a single soldier.

Thomas Parran Jr.

Thomas Parran Jr. served the longest term in office. He was surgeon general for 12 years, from 1936 to 1948.

Jocelyn Elders, the second woman to become surgeon general, had the shortest term in office. She served from September 8, 1993, to December 31, 1994, under President Bill Clinton.

Antonia C. Novello served as surgeon general from 1990 to 1993. She was the first woman and the first Hispanic American to hold the post. She was also the first surgeon general not born in one of the 50 states. Novello was born and raised in Fajardo, Puerto Rico.

Jocelyn Elders

David Satcher was the first African-American man to serve as surgeon general, from 1998 to 2002. He was also the first person to hold the posts of surgeon general and assistant secretary for health at the same time. He served in both positions from 1998 to 2001.

David Satcher (right) was the first African-American surgeon general.

Glossary

adviser—a person who works closely with a person in power and provides information and suggestions

boycott—to join together and agree not to buy from or sell to another person, business, or nation

cholera—a disease of the stomach and intestine that is very contagious

commissioned—a written order giving authority to a person or group of people

contagious—easily spread from one person to another

corps—a group of soldiers trained for special military service

dietitian—a person trained to plan meals that have the right amount of various kinds of food

emphysema—a disease of the lungs that makes breathing difficult

epidemic—the rapid spread of a disease so that many people have it at the same time

pharmacist—a person licensed to fill prescription drugs

quarantine—to keep away from others for a time to prevent the spread of a disease

smallpox—a contagious disease that causes fever and red spots on the skin

therapist—a person who specializes in the treatment of some kind of disease

Surgeon General Antonia Novello held a press conference in 1992 on a new national health program for Hispanic Americans.

For More Information

Publications

Feinberg, Barbara Silberdick. *The National Government.* . New York: Franklin Watts, 1993.

Web Sites

www.surgeongeneral.gov/sgoffice.htm

Web site of the surgeon general's office. Includes health tips and links about the history of the surgeon general's office, and individual biographies of the 16 men and women who have held the post since 1871.

www.usphs.gov

Web site of the Commissioned Corps. Includes information on the jobs the corps performs, its history, and how to join the corps.

Index